Vultures

by Roland Smith
photographs by Lynn M. Stone

Lerner Publications Company • Minneapolis, Minnesota

For Michael Roydon. You owe me a dollar!
                                          —RS

A book for Brittany, who much prefers cats to vultures, but whose heart is big enough to embrace all creatures.

                                          —LMS

Thanks to our series consultant, Sharyn Fenwick, elementary science / math specialist. Mrs. Fenwick was the winner of the National Science Teachers Association 1991 Distinguished Teaching Award. She also was the recipient of the Presidential Award for Excellence in Math and Science Teaching, representing the state of Minnesota at the elementary level in 1992.

Additional photos are reproduced through the courtesy of: p. 27, © Andrea Gaski / Ron Tilson, Oklahoma City Zoo; pp. 30–32, © Richard Day / Daybreak Imagery; p. 33, © Michael P. Turco; p. 34, © Joe McDonald; p. 38, N. Snyder / USFWS; pp. 39–41, Ron Garrison, © Zoological Society of San Diego.

Early Bird Nature Books were conceptualized by Ruth Berman and designed by Steve Foley. Series editor is Joelle Goldman.

Text copyright © 1997 by Roland Smith
Photographs copyright © 1997 by Lynn M. Stone, except where noted

Library of Congress Cataloging-in-Publication Data

Smith, Roland, 1951–
    Vultures / by Roland Smith ; photographs by Lynn M. Stone.
       p.   cm. — (Early bird nature books)
    Includes index.
    Summary: Describes the life cycle, behavior, eating habits, and endangered status of vultures.
       ISBN 0-8225-3011-2 (alk. paper)
       1. Vultures—Juvenile literature. [1. Vultures. 2. Endangered species.] I. Stone, Lynn M., ill. II. Title. III. Series.
QL696.F32S58 1997
598.9'2—DC21   96-47074

Manufactured in the United States of America
1 2 3 4 5 6 – SP – 02 01 00 99 98 97

Contents

Alaska
(U.S.)

CANADA

UNITED STATES

Vultures live all over the world. The striped areas show where vultures can be found in North America.

MEXICO

Be a Word Detective

Can you find these words as you read about the vulture's life? Be a detective and try to figure out what they mean. You can turn to the glossary on page 46 for help.

carcasses	germs	raptors
carrion	habitats	regurgitate
down feathers	incubating	scavengers
extinct	nests	soaring

Chapter 1

The hooded vulture lives in Africa. How many kinds of vultures are there in the world?

A Variety of Vultures

Vultures are big birds who have only a few feathers on their heads. Vultures eat dead animals. Because vultures look strange and they have odd eating habits, some people don't like them. But vultures are important. They help to keep the world clean.

The king vulture is one of the most colorful vultures. It lives in the forests of South America.

There are 22 species, or kinds, of vultures. They live in many different places. The kinds of places where vultures can live are called their habitats. Deserts, rain forests, and cities are habitats for vultures. You might even see vultures flying above your neighborhood.

Vultures come in many sizes. The largest vultures are the condors. Their wings are 10 feet across from tip to tip. Condors weigh about 25 pounds. They are the largest birds on earth who can fly.

Andean condors live in the Andes Mountains. These mountains run along the western coast of South America.

8

An Egyptian vulture is about 2 feet long from head to tail. Egyptian vultures live in Africa, Asia, and Europe.

The smallest vulture is the Egyptian (ee-JIP-shuhn) vulture. It weighs only 3 or 4 pounds. That's about as much as a chicken weighs.

Chapter 2

Most vultures eat meat. What kinds of birds are related to vultures?

Garbage Collectors

 Vultures are related to eagles, hawks, and owls. Vultures, eagles, hawks, and owls are called raptors. Most birds eat seeds, insects, or plants. Raptors eat other animals. They are meat eaters.

Most raptors have strong feet. Their toes are tipped with sharp claws. They can swoop down and use their feet to grab a small animal. Then they can kill the animal with a swift squeeze of their feet. Most vultures can't kill with their feet, because their feet are weak.

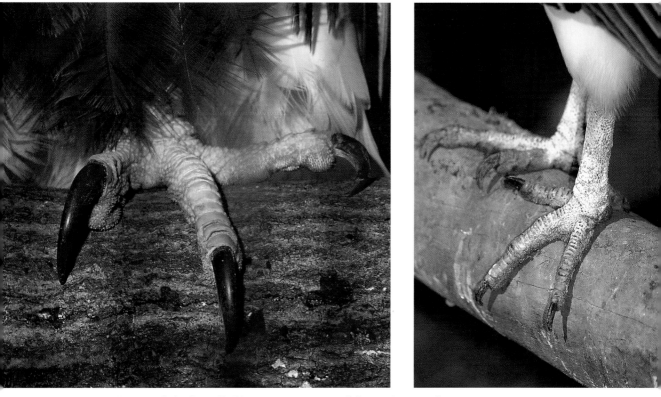

An eagle's feet (left) *are strong and have large claws. A vulture's feet* (right) *are weak. A vulture's feet are made for hopping around on the ground, not for killing.*

These white-backed vultures have found some animals who drowned in a river.

Most vultures do not kill animals. They find carcasses to eat. A carcass is the body of an animal who has died. The meat on a carcass is called carrion. Animals who eat carrion are called scavengers (SKAV-uhn-jurz).

Scavengers are nature's garbage collectors. By eating carrion, they clean up the earth.

Vultures are perfectly made for eating carrion. Most vultures have only a few feathers on their heads. If a vulture's head had more feathers, blood would get under them when the bird ate carrion. Having fewer feathers helps a vulture to stay clean.

A lappet-faced vulture has only a few small feathers on its head and neck.

Germs (jurmz) grow in rotting meat. Some germs can make animals sick. But vultures can eat rotting carrion without getting sick. They have tough stomachs. They are not hurt by the germs and poisons in rotting meat.

These birds are turkey vultures. Some people call turkey vultures "buzzards." But vultures are different from buzzards. A buzzard is a kind of hawk.

A spotted hyena is chasing vultures away from a dead animal.

Sometimes a vulture is attacked by another animal, such as a hyena or coyote. The vulture has a special way of protecting itself. It throws up on its enemy! The food from a vulture's stomach smells terrible. When a vulture throws up, it usually scares its enemy away. If the enemy doesn't leave, the vulture falls down on the ground and pretends to be dead.

Chapter 3

A vulture's wide wings help it glide through the air. Vultures spend most of their time flying high in the sky. How do they find food?

Finding Food

Vultures search for food while they are flying. They don't flap their wings much when they fly. Instead, they glide like a kite. This way of flying is called soaring. Vultures do not have to work hard when they soar. They can stay up in the air for hours.

Most birds have good eyesight. But they usually have a poor sense of smell. So most vultures use their sharp eyesight to find carrion. But turkey vultures and yellow-headed vultures have a good sense of smell. They can smell carrion from high in the sky.

Turkey vultures use their sense of smell to find food. They can find a dead animal even if it is hidden under a tree. The turkey vulture's scientific name is Cathartes aura.

As vultures look for food, they watch for animals who are hurt or sick. If a vulture finds a hurt animal, it soars in a circle high above the animal. It waits to see if the animal will die. If the animal dies, the vulture flies down to eat.

Vultures fly far above the ground. They can see a dead animal when they are 2 miles above it.

These vultures see a hurt or dead animal. They are flying in a circle high above it.

19

Many vultures are waiting for a hyena to finish its meal. Then the vultures will eat.

Some vultures get their food from humans. These vultures don't soar over the countryside, searching for something to eat. They live near garbage dumps and other places where people throw away a lot of food.

A black vulture has found a dead opossum. The scientific name of the black vulture is Coragyps atratus.

Vultures also eat animals that have been hit and killed by cars. These dead animals are called roadkill. As vultures eat roadkill, they have to look out for cars. Otherwise, they may become roadkill themselves!

Chapter 4

While some vultures eat, others wait nearby. How many vultures may come to eat from a carcass?

Table Manners

 When one vulture finds a carcass, other vultures soon arrive. Over 200 vultures may gather around one carcass.

Vultures' table manners are not the best. Vultures squabble and peck. They try to chase each other away. Smaller vultures have to wait until bigger vultures have eaten. This is not a problem, though. Different kinds of vultures eat differently.

Vultures fight to get bits of meat from a dead animal.

All vultures have hooked beaks that are made for tearing meat. But vultures use their beaks in different ways.

Large vultures, such as the Indian king vulture, rarely stick their heads inside a carcass. Their beaks can cut through tough skin. These vultures eat the tough meat that is just under a carcass's skin.

The cinereous vulture is the largest vulture in Europe and Asia. A cinereous vulture doesn't put its head inside carcasses, so it doesn't get blood on its neck feathers.

A Rüppell's griffon vulture is reaching inside a dead animal. Its long neck has few feathers to get messy.

Griffon vultures are medium-sized. They have very long necks. Their beaks are made for pulling. They can snake their heads deep inside large carcasses and pull out soft meat.

The small Egyptian vulture has a beak made for pecking small bits of meat from bones. It has to wait for other scavengers to cut through the carcass's skin before it can eat.

Vultures have cleaned the last bits of meat from a dead animal. Only the bones are left.

Vultures are not picky about the food they eat. Almost any dead animal will do. But if they have a choice, vultures would rather eat fresh meat than rotten meat.

Meat is not the only food vultures eat. Egyptian vultures often eat ostrich eggs. But ostrich eggs are hard to crack. An Egyptian vulture knows how to crack ostrich eggs. It picks up rocks with its beak. It throws rocks at the egg until it breaks open. Then the vulture can eat the egg.

An Egyptian vulture is holding a rock in its beak. The vulture will throw the rock at the ostrich egg to crack it open.

The bearded vulture eats bones! It swallows small bones whole. But some bones are too large to swallow. The vulture picks up a large bone and flies into the air. The bird drops the bone on rocks, over and over, until it breaks. Then the vulture licks out the soft center of the bone.

Bearded vultures live in the mountains in parts of Europe, Africa, and Asia.

These black vultures and turkey vultures are resting together in a tree. Black vultures and turkey vultures live in North America and South America.

Large vultures eat a lot of food at one time. They can wait a long time between meals. Small vultures eat small amounts of food. They need to eat more often than large vultures.

Chapter 5

Some vultures lay their eggs on the ground. These are a turkey vulture's eggs. How long does it take for a vulture's egg to hatch?

Baby Vultures

Some kinds of vultures make nests out of sticks. They usually build them in the branches of trees or along cliffs. Other kinds of vultures don't use sticks to make their nests. These vultures nest inside hollow trees or on rocky ledges.

Condors and king vultures lay only one egg at a time. But most species of vultures lay two eggs. Male and female vultures take turns incubating (ING-kyuh-bay-ting) their eggs by sitting on them. They incubate the eggs to keep them warm. It takes five to eight weeks for the eggs to hatch.

A black vulture is sitting on her eggs to keep them warm.

Vulture chicks are covered with fluffy down feathers. The feathers range in color from snowy white to brown. After several weeks, adult feathers begin to grow.

These turkey vulture chicks are only two or three days old. They are covered with fluffy white down feathers.

These black vulture chicks are in their nest inside a hollow tree. The chicks' adult feathers have begun to grow.

Young vulture chicks depend on their parents for food. Vulture parents carry food to the nest in their stomachs. At first, parents regurgitate (ree-GUR-juh-tate) the food. They throw up into the chicks' throats. When the chicks get stronger, they eat out of their parents' mouths. Later, the parents bring scraps of meat to the nest in their beaks. Or they regurgitate food into the nest for the chicks to eat.

This young lappet-faced vulture (left) will soon leave the nest. It will stay with its parents until it has learned how to find food.

Chicks stay in the nest until they are ready to fly. Turkey vultures can fly when they are two and a half months old. Condors learn to fly when they are six or seven months old. When the young vultures can fly, they follow their parents. Their parents teach them how to find carrion.

As this young king vulture grows up, its head will become brightly colored. Can you find a picture of an adult king vulture in this book?

Chapter 6

There are many African white-backed vultures, but some kinds of vultures are in danger. How do people make it hard for some vultures to live?

Saving Vultures

  There are not as many vultures as there used to be. Some species of vultures are nearly extinct. When a species is extinct, it is gone forever.

There are many reasons why vultures are dying. Their habitat may be destroyed by people. Then the vultures have nowhere to live. Some vultures are poisoned by sprays used to kill insects. Other vultures land on electrical wires and are shocked to death. And ranchers sometimes shoot vultures because they think vultures kill their animals.

Cinereous vultures once lived in most of Europe. Many of them died. Most of the ones who are left live in southern Europe.

The California condor is one of the rarest birds on earth. As humans moved into condor habitats, many condors were shot or poisoned. Not many chicks were born. By 1980, very few condors were left.

In 1987, biologists captured all of the California condors that were left in the wild. The biologists put the giant vultures in zoos.

California condors once lived in most of North America, but only a few of them are left. The scientific name of the California condor is Gymnogyps californianus.

California condor parents usually have only one chick every two years. People are helping this condor chick hatch out of its egg.

Capturing the condors was the only way to save them from becoming extinct.

Scientists want more condors to hatch each year. When a condor lays an egg, scientists take it away. Then the bird lays another one. Scientists can fool condors into laying two or three eggs a year!

The scientists put the condor eggs that they have taken into an incubator. The incubator keeps the eggs warm. When the chicks hatch, zookeepers take care of them.

People are keeping this newly hatched California condor chick warm.

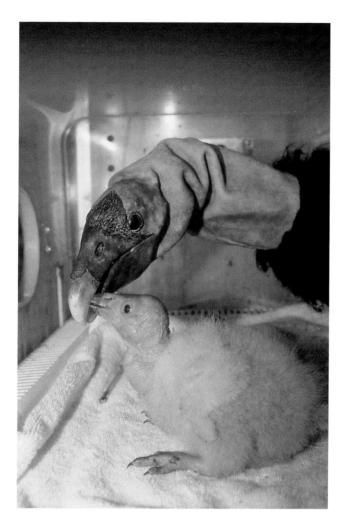

Zookeepers use puppets that look like a condor's head to feed condor chicks.

Zoos have hatched over 70 condor chicks. In 1992, zoos began freeing condors who had been raised by humans. The birds were released into a forest in California. In time, many more condors will be freed.

The Eurasian griffon vulture lives in parts of Europe, Asia, and Africa.

People are also trying to save other vultures. "Vulture restaurants" have been set up in Europe, Africa, and North America. People leave animal carcasses in special feeding places. Then vultures can eat the carcasses.

Some ranchers know that vultures are valuable. Vultures clean up carrion and keep germs from spreading. Vultures also help

ranchers find dead or hurt animals. All the
rancher has to do is look up in the air. If
vultures are circling, a dead or hurt animal
is nearby.

Without vultures soaring high overhead,
who will keep our world clean? We need these
wonderful scavengers in the sky.

Vultures are important. They help to keep the world clean.

On Sharing a Book

As you know, adults greatly influence a child's attitude toward reading. When a child sees you read, or when you share a book with a child, you're sending a message that reading is important. Show the child that reading a book together is important to you. Find a comfortable, quiet place. Turn off the television and limit other distractions, such as telephone calls.

Be prepared to start slowly. Take turns reading parts of this book. Stop and talk about what you're reading. Talk about the photographs. You may find that much of the shared time is spent discussing just a few pages. This discussion time is valuable for both of you, so don't move through the book too quickly. If the child begins to lose interest, stop reading. Continue sharing the book at another time. When you do pick up the book again, be sure to revisit the parts you have already read. Most importantly, enjoy the book!

Be a Vocabulary Detective

You will find a word list on page 5. Words selected for this list are important to the understanding of the topic of this book. Encourage the child to be a word detective and search for the words as you read the book together. Talk about what the words mean and how they are used in the sentence. Do any of these words have more than one meaning? You will find these words defined in a glossary on page 46.

What about Questions?

Use questions to make sure the child understands the information in this book. Here are some suggestions:

> What did this paragraph tell us? What does this picture show? What do you think we'll learn about next? Could a vulture live in your neighborhood? Why/Why not? How do vultures find food? How do vultures protect themselves from enemies? Why do vultures sometimes fly in a circle high in the sky? How is a vulture family like your family and how is it different? What do you think it's like being a vulture? What is your favorite part of the book? Why?

If the child has questions, don't hesitate to respond with questions of your own, such as: What do *you* think? Why? What is it that you don't know? If the child can't remember certain facts, turn to the index.

Introducing the Index

The index is an important learning tool. It helps readers get information quickly without searching throughout the whole book. Turn to the index on page 47. Choose an entry, such as *beaks,* and ask the child to use the index to find out how vultures use their beaks. Repeat this exercise with as many entries as you like. Ask the child to point out the differences between an index and a glossary. (The index helps readers find information quickly, while the glossary tells readers what words mean.)

Where in the World?

Many plants and animals found in the Early Bird Nature Books series live in parts of the world other than the United States. Encourage the child to find the places mentioned in this book on a world map or globe. Take time to talk about climate, terrain, and how you might live in such places.

All the World in Metric!

Although our monetary system is in metric units (based on multiples of 10), the United States is one of the few countries in the world that does not use the metric system of measurement. Here are some conversion activities you and the child can do using a calculator:

WHEN YOU KNOW:	MULTIPLY BY:	TO FIND:
miles	1.609	kilometers
feet	0.3048	meters
inches	2.54	centimeters
gallons	3.787	liters
tons	0.907	metric tons
pounds	0.454	kilograms

Activities

The Egyptian vulture is sometimes called "Pharaoh's chicken." Do you know why? Go to the library and find out about the pharaohs of Egypt.

Visit a zoo to see vultures and other raptors. How are the raptors similar to other kinds of birds in the zoo and how are they different?

Vultures' big wings help them soar high in the sky like a kite. Buy or make a kite. Fly your kite in an open area, away from trees and power lines. Does your kite fly better near the ground, or high in the air?

Glossary

carcasses—the bodies of dead animals

carrion—the meat on a dead animal's body

down feathers—soft, fluffy feathers

extinct—no members of a kind of animal are still living

germs (jurmz)—very small living things. Some germs can make animals sick.

habitats—areas where a kind of animal can live and grow

incubating (ING-kyuh-bay-ting)—sitting on eggs and keeping them warm so they will hatch

nests—places where birds lay their eggs and bring up their babies

raptors—birds who eat meat

regurgitate—to bring food from the stomach back into the mouth

scavengers (SKAV-uhn-jurz)—animals who find and eat dead animals

soaring—flying high in the air without working hard

Index

Pages listed in **bold** type refer to photographs.

About the Author

In his career, Roland Smith has been a zoo keeper, senior zoo keeper, curator of mammals and birds, general curator, assistant zoo director, and senior research biologist. Roland has appeared on several local and national television shows, including the National Geographic special called *Elephants*. He has written other books for children, including *Sea Otter Rescue, Inside the Zoo Nursery, Thunder Cave,* and *Jaguar.* He is the author of *African Elephants,* another title in Lerner's Early Bird Nature Books series. Roland and his wife, Marie, live on a small farm in Stafford, Oregon.

About the Photographer

Lynn M. Stone is an author and photographer who has written more than 250 books for young readers about wildlife and natural history. He is the author and photographer of *Cougars, Penguins, Sandhill Cranes,* and *Swans,* and the photographer for *Tigers,* all titles in Lerner's Early Bird Nature Books series. In addition to photographing wildlife, Mr. Stone enjoys fishing and traveling. A former teacher, he lives with his wife and daughter in Batavia, Illinois.

48